Quick & Easy Vegetarian Rice Cooker Meals

Over 50 recipes for breakfast, main dishes, and desserts

By Susan Evans

Copyright © 2015 Susan Evans

All rights reserved. This book or any portion thereof may not be reproduced or used in any manner whatsoever without the express written permission of the publisher except for the use of brief quotations in a book review.

Other popular books by Susan Evans

Vegetarian Mediterranean Cookbook:
Over 50 recipes for appetizers, salads, dips, and main dishes

Quick & Easy Asian Vegetarian Cookbook:
Over 50 recipes for stir fries, rice, noodles, and appetizers

Vegetarian Slow Cooker Cookbook:
Over 75 recipes for meals, soups, stews, desserts, and sides

Quick & Easy Vegan Desserts Cookbook:
Over 80 delicious recipes for cakes, cupcakes, brownies, cookies, fudge, pies, candy, and so much more!

Quick & Easy Microwave Meals:
Over 50 recipes for breakfast, snacks, meals and desserts

Halloween Cookbook:
80 Ghoulish recipes for appetizers, meals, drinks, and desserts

FREE BONUS!

Would you like to receive one of my cookbooks for free? Just leave me on honest review on Amazon and I will send you a digital version of the cookbook of your choice! All you have to do is email me proof of your review and the desired cookbook and format to susan.evans.author@gmail.com. Thank you for your support, and have fun cooking!

Introduction 1

Measurement Conversions 2

Breakfast 3

Frittata with Summer Vegetables *4*
Vanilla Almond Steel-Cut Oatmeal *5*
Avocado Breakfast Bowl *6*
Rice Cooker Oatmeal...*7*
Creamy Grits..*8*
Steel Cut Oats *9*
Creamy Oatmeal *10*
Tapioca Pudding..*11*

Rice Dishes...12

Dill and Lemon Rice with Feta..*13*
Spanish Rice *14*
Fragrant Basmati Rice *15*
Carrots and Peas Rice *16*
Lemon Rice..*17*
Orange Chipotle Risotto *18*
Moroccan Brown Rice..*19*
Rice Pilaf..*20*
Mexican Rice *21*
Italian Rice and Peas *22*
Caribbean Rice *23*
Mexican Green Rice..*24*
Easy Coconut Rice...*25*
Vegetable Rice Pilaf..*26*

Quick and Easy Spinach Rice..27
Chile Cheese Rice..28
Toasted Coconut Yellow Rice...29
Wild Berry Rice 30
Brown Rice with Miso 31
Saffron & Fruit Chutney Yellow Rice...................................32
Sushi Rice 33
Rice and Black Beans..34
Easy Jambalaya Curry 35
Polynesian Rice 36
Quick and Easy Curry Rice...37

NON-RICE DISHES 38

Rice Cooker Mac & Cheese 39
Very Cheesy Polenta..40
Steamed Tofu & Asparagus 41
Southwest-Style Quinoa 42
Kimchi...43
Rice Cooker Quinoa 44
Cheesy Paprika Mac 'n Cheese..45
Pasta Cubano..46
Quinoa Pomegranate salad...47
Potato Salad...48
Black Bean Chili 49
Rice Cooker Polenta..50
Rice Cooker Quinoa 51
Jamaican Grits 52

DESSERTS 53

Gingerbread Cake..54

Rice Pudding..*55*
Coconut-Pecan Upside Down Cake................................*56*
Apple Rice Pudding...*57*
Chocolate Cake..*58*

THANK YOU **59**

INTRODUCTION

The rice cooker is the perfect home appliance for cooking, and the simplest way to make meals. No longer do you need to worry about burnt rice or having to keep an eye on a pot on the stove. Just pop in some rice and water, hit the cook button and let it go. You get hot and soft rice every time all the time. Plus, preparation and cleanup is left to the absolute minimum.

Rice cookers are a time-saving replacement for traditional cooking and can be used for a lot more than just rice. This includes cakes, oatmeal, pastas, and so much more! Stop being dissatisfied with the same old vegetarian recipes or looking up new ones that are just tedious and confusing, and prepare your taste buds for a splendidly delicious adventure! This cookbook contains over 50 delectable recipes for breakfast, rice meals, non-rice main dishes, and desserts that will surprise yourself and others. So plug in that rice cooker and let's start cooking!

*The following recipes can be used on simple rice cookers with only an on/off button to more advanced types. The rice cooker should be at least 4 cups capacity, and recipes should be adjust accordingly if smaller. Unless otherwise stated all ingredients should be measured using standard measuring cups instead of the rice cooker cup.

MEASUREMENT CONVERSIONS

Liquid/Volume Measurements (approximate)

1 teaspoon = 1/6 fluid ounce (oz.) = 1/3 tablespoon = 5 ml

1 tablespoon = 1/2 fluid ounce (oz.) = 3 teaspoons = 15 ml

1 fluid ounce (oz.) = 2 tablespoons = 1/8 cup = 30 ml

1/4 cup = 2 fluid ounces (oz.) = 4 tablespoons = 60 ml

1/3 cup = 2⅔ fluid ounces (oz.) = 5 ⅓ tablespoons = 80 ml

1/2 cup = 4 fluid ounces (oz.) = 8 tablespoons = 120 ml

2/3 cup = 5⅓ fluid ounces (oz.) = 10⅔ tablespoons = 160 ml

3/4 cup = 6 fluid ounces (oz.) = 12 tablespoons = 180 ml

7/8 cup = 7 fluid ounces (oz.) = 14 tablespoons = 210 ml

1 cup = 8 fluid ounces (oz.) = 1/2 pint = 240 ml

1 pint = 16 fluid ounces (oz.) = 2 cups = 1/2 quart = 475 ml

1 quart = 4 cups = 32 fluid ounces (oz.) = 2 pints = 950 ml

1 liter = 1.055 quarts = 4.22 cups = 2.11 pints = 1000 ml

1 gallon = 4 quarts = 8 pints = 3.8 liters

Dry/Weight Measurements (approximate)

1 ounce (oz.) = 30 grams (g)

2 ounces (oz.) = 55 grams (g)

3 ounces (oz.) = 85 grams (g)

1/4 pound (lb.) = 4 ounces (oz.) = 125 grams (g)

1/2 pound (lb.) = 8 ounces (oz.) = 240 grams (g)

3/4 pound (lb.) = 12 ounces (oz.) = 375 grams (g)

1 pound (lb.) = 16 ounces (oz.) = 455 grams (g)

2 pounds (lbs.) = 32 ounces (oz.) = 910 grams (g)

1 kilogram (kg) = 2.2 pounds (lbs.) = 1000 gram (g)

BREAKFAST

Frittata with Summer Vegetables

SERVINGS: 4
PREP TIME: 5 min.
TOTAL TIME: 50 min

Ingredients

- 1 whole garlic clove, peeled
- 1 small red or yellow pepper, cut into small dice
- 1 small potato, peeled and finely julienned
- 1 small zucchini, sliced into thin rounds salt and pepper
- 1 tablespoon olive oil
- 6 large eggs
- 2 tablespoons grated cheese of any kind (optional)
- salt and pepper
- 1 tablespoon olive oil

Instructions

1. Heat frying pan with 1 tablespoon of olive oil. Add garlic clove and cook until garlic is lightly brown. Discard the garlic clove. Add the vegetables. Season with salt and pepper and set aside.
2. Put 1 tablespoon of olive oil in the rice cooker. Spread it around the bottom and up the sides with a paper towel. Add eggs, grated cheese, salt and pepper, and beat the eggs in the bowl (avoid scratching the rice cooker). Add the vegetables and distribute evenly in the egg mixture.
3. Put bowl in rice cooker and switch to Cook.
4. When it finishes cooking, let cool completely and cut into wedges.

Vanilla Almond Steel-Cut Oatmeal

SERVINGS: 3
PREP TIME: 10 min.
TOTAL TIME: 40 min.

Ingredients

- 1 cup steel-cut oats
- 2 cups unsweetened, original soy milk
- 1 1/2 cup water
- 2 teaspoons vanilla extract
- 1/2 teaspoon salt
- raw sliced almonds
- brown sugar
- maple syrup

Instructions

1. Add oatmeal, soymilk, water, vanilla extract, and salt to rice cooker. Set to porridge setting or regular Cook setting.
2. Add toppings and serve.

Avocado Breakfast Bowl

SERVINGS: 2
PREP TIME: 10 min.
TOTAL TIME: 30 min.

Ingredients

- 1/2 cup water
- 1/4 cup red quinoa
- 1 1/2 teaspoons olive oil
- 2 eggs
- 1 pinch salt and ground black pepper to taste
- 1/4 teaspoon seasoned salt
- 1/4 teaspoon ground black pepper
- 1 avocado, diced
- 2 tablespoons crumbled feta cheese

Instructions

1. Combine water and quinoa together in a rice cooker. Cook until quinoa is tender, around 15 minutes.
2. Heat olive oil in a skillet over medium heat. Cook eggs as desired an; season with salt and pepper.
3. Combine quinoa and eggs in a bowl.
4. Top with avocado and feta cheese.

Rice Cooker Oatmeal

SERVINGS: 3
PREP TIME: 5 min.
TOTAL TIME: 30 min.

Ingredients

- 1 1/4 cups large flake rolled oats
- 2 tablespoons wheat bran
- 1 pinch salt
- 1/3 cup raisins or 1/3 cup fresh or dried fruit (optional)
- 2 1/2 cups water

Instructions

1. Put all ingredients in a rice cooker and turn on. It should be done around 25 to 30 minutes. Stir once during cooking.
2. Sprinkle with some ground flaxseed, sugar, and light cream; if desired.

Creamy Grits

SERVINGS: 2
PREP TIME: 5 min.
TOTAL TIME: 30 min.

Ingredients

- 1/2 cup stone-ground grits
- 1 1/2 cups milk
- 1/4 teaspoon salt
- 1 tablespoon butter
- Spoonful of cherry

Instructions

1. Put all ingredients into rice cooker bowl and combine. Set to Cook. Stir after 10 minutes into cycle.
2. Serve with a pat of butter and a spoonful of cherry or other preserves.

Steel Cut Oats

SERVINGS: 4
PREP TIME: 5 min.
TOTAL TIME: 25 min.

Ingredients

- 1 part steel cut oats
- 3 parts water
- pinch of salt

Instructions

1. Put oats, water and salt in rice cooker. Try to add up to half the capacity of rice cooker, since oats bubble up more than rice.
2. Start rice cooker.

Creamy Oatmeal

SERVINGS: 2
PREP TIME: 5 min.
TOTAL TIME: 30 min

Ingredients

- 2/3 cup steel cut oats
- 1 2/3 cups milk
- 1 teaspoon pure vanilla extract
- 1 1/4 teaspoons ground cinnamon
- 1 pinch fine sea salt
- 2 tablespoons pure maple syrup
- 1/2 cup chopped dates

Instructions

1. Place all ingredients except dates, in rice cooker. Gently stir to combine and sprinkle dates on top. Cover and set on Porridge cycle, or set to Cook if rice cooker doesn't have one. Watch to determine when the oatmeal is done, around 25 to 30 minutes.

Tapioca Pudding

SERVINGS: 4
PREP TIME: 5 min.
TOTAL TIME: 25 min

Ingredients

- 3 tablespoons small pearl tapioca
- 2 cups milk
- 1 large egg
- 1/2 cup sugar
- 1 pinch salt
- 1 teaspoon pure vanilla extract

Instructions

1. Place tapioca in rice cooker. In a small bowl, whisk together milk, egg, sugar, and salt. Pour milk mix over the tapioca and stir to combine. Cover and set to Porridge cycle or to Cook for 20 minutes.
2. When it switches to Warm cycle, remove bowl from cooker and stir in vanilla. Pour pudding into a large bowl or individual dishes.
3. Let cool.
4. Serve warm, if desired, or refrigerate covered with plastic wrap.

RICE DISHES

Dill and Lemon Rice with Feta

SERVINGS: 3
PREP TIME: 5 min.
TOTAL TIME: 45 min.

Ingredients

- 1 1/2 cups long grain white rice
- 2 cups vegetable stock
- 2 tablespoons olive oil
- 2 small boiling onions, chopped
- 1/4 cup pine nuts
- 1/4 cup fresh lemon juice
- 1 tablespoon minced fresh dill
- 1 1/2 teaspoons minced of fresh mint, optional
- 1 cup crumbled feta
- 1 lemon, cut in 8 wedges

Instructions

1. Coat rice bowl with cooking spray. Add rice and stock. Set for the regular white rice cycle.
2. When it switches to Warm, let stand and steam for 10 minutes.
3. Heat olive oil in a small skillet. Add onions and cook for 5 minutes, frequently stirring until soft. Add pine nuts. Cook and stir until golden, about a minute.
4. Add the onion and pine nut mixture to the rice, along with the lemon juice, dill, and mint (if using). Stir with a plastic rice paddle or a wooden spoon to combine.
5. Cover and continue on Warm setting for 10 more minutes.
6. Transfer to a serving dish, and top with the feta and lemon wedges.

Spanish Rice

SERVINGS: 8
PREP TIME: 10 min.
TOTAL TIME: 40 min

Ingredients

- 2 cups long grain rice
- 1 cup water
- 1 (8 ounce) can tomato sauce
- 14 ounces Mexican-style stewed tomatoes, with juice
- 1/4 cup salsa
- 3/4 teaspoon cumin
- 2 teaspoons chili powder
- 3/4 teaspoon garlic salt
- 1 1/2 teaspoons dried onion
- 3/4 teaspoon salt, optional
- 1/2 cup water
- 1 small green pepper, diced, optional
- 1 (4 ounce) can diced green chilies, optional

Instructions

1. Spray rice cooker with cooking spray. Add and stir in rice, 1 cup water, and all other ingredients.
2. When the cycle is almost completed check the rice and add additional 1/2 cup water if necessary. The amount of water will differ depending on what kind of rice you use.
3. Serve warm.

Fragrant Basmati Rice

SERVINGS: 3
PREP TIME: 15 min.
TOTAL TIME: 35 min.

Ingredients

- 1 cup basmati rice
- 1 1/2 cups water
- 1/4 teaspoon salt
- 1 cinnamon stick (4 inches)
- 3 green cardamom pods

Instructions

1. Rinse the rice and thoroughly drain. Place all ingredients in the rice cooker and stir to combine. Set regular Cook cycle.
2. When the machine shifts to Warm, set a timer for 15 minutes. When done, fluff rice with the plastic or wooden paddle/spoon.
3. Serve warm.

Carrots and Peas Rice

SERVINGS: 6
PREP TIME: 10 min.
TOTAL TIME: 35 min.

Ingredients

- 2 tablespoons unsalted butter, divided
- 1/4 cup carrot, sliced in rounds
- 1 1/2 cups long grain white rice (or any flavorful white rice)
- 2 cups vegetable stock
- 1 tablespoon fresh Italian parsley, chopped
- 1 teaspoon dried thyme
- 1/4 cup frozen peas
- 1 tablespoon almonds, chopped

Instructions

1. In a small skillet over medium heat, melt 1 tablespoon of butter. Add the carrots stir and cook, until softened, around 2-3 minutes.
2. Place rice in rice cooker. Add and stir in stock, parsley, thyme, peas and sautéed carrots. Close cover and press Cook. When machine switches to Warm, let rice steam for 10 minutes.
3. Fluff rice with wooden spoon. When ready to serve, add 1 tablespoon of butter and almonds. Stir and immediately serve.

Lemon Rice

SERVINGS: 4
PREP/ TOTAL TIME: 45 min.

Ingredients

- 1 cup long grain rice
- 1 1/2 cups vegetable stock
- 1 pinch salt
- 1 large garlic clove
- 2 teaspoons lemon zest, freshly grated
- 2 tablespoons unsalted butter
- 2 tablespoons fresh Italian parsley

Instructions

1. Place rinsed rice in the rice cooker bowl. Add chicken stock and salt and stir to combine. Place the garlic on top of the rice in the center.
2. Close the cover and set to Cook. When it switches to the Warm, add and stir in lemon zest, butter, and parsley. Close cover and let the rice steam for 10 minutes. Fluff with a rice paddle.
3. Before serving, remove and discard garlic. Serve hot.

Orange Chipotle Risotto

SERVINGS: 6
PREP TIME: 10 min.
TOTAL TIME: 45 min.

Ingredients

- 1 tablespoon butter
- 1 small onion (about 1 cup)
- 1 cup Arborio rice
- 3 cups hot water, adding more if needed
- 1 cup orange juice
- 1/2 teaspoon orange zest
- 1 teaspoon saffron thread, optional
- 1 chipotle chile in adobo, to taste
- 3 ounces asiago cheese, 1/2 cup grated
- 1 bunch fresh parsley, 1/4 cup chopped

Instructions

1. Sauté onions in butter in an open rice cooker.
2. Add Arborio rice and liquids, zest, saffron, and chipotle pepper and sauce. Set to Cook.
3. Mix in grated cheese and herbs after it has switched to Warm cycle.
4. Season to taste with salt and pepper.

Moroccan Brown Rice

SERVINGS: 4
PREP TIME: 5 min.
TOTAL TIME: 45 min.

Ingredients

- 1 1/2 cups long grain brown rice
- 2 3/4 cups water or 2 3/4 cups vegetable stock
- 3/4 teaspoon salt
- 1/2 teaspoon pepper
- 1 teaspoon ground coriander
- 1/2 teaspoon ground cardamom
- 3 tablespoons butter, cut into pieces
- 1/4 cup preserved lemon, minced, garnish

Instructions

1. Coat rice cooker bowl with cooking spray. Place rice in the bowl and add water, salt, pepper, coriander and cardamom.
2. Cover and set the Brown rice cycle. Add the butter when the machine switches to Warm.
3. Cover and let rice steam for 10 minutes.
4. Fluff rice and serve hot. Sprinkled some preserved lemon.

Rice Pilaf

SERVINGS: 7
PREP TIME: 10 min.
TOTAL TIME: 25 min

Ingredients

- 1 1/2 cups white rice
- 2 cups vegetable broth
- 1/4 cup slivered almonds
- 1 cup sliced mushrooms
- 1/2 small onion, diced
- 2 teaspoons margarine or 2 teaspoons butter
- 2 teaspoons minced garlic cloves

Instructions

1. In a small frying pan, sauté onion and garlic over medium heat until onion is translucent.
2. Add rice, sautéed onion and garlic, almonds, mushrooms, and broth to rice cooker. Stir and set to cook.
3. When finished cooking, let sit for 10 minutes.

Mexican Rice

SERVINGS: 6
PREP/TOTAL TIME: 25 min.

Ingredients

- 1 cup rice
- 2 1/4 cups low sodium vegetable broth
- 6 ounce tomato paste
- 2 tablespoons butter
- 1/2 cup onion, diced
- 1 garlic clove, small, minced
- 4 ounces diced green chilies
- 1 dash pepper
- 1 dash red pepper flakes
- cilantro or parsley

Instructions

1. Combine and stir in ingredients in rice cooker. Press cook.
2. When cooking is finished let stand uncovered for 3 minutes.
3. Stir before serving.

Italian Rice and Peas

SERVINGS: 5
PREP TIME: 15 min.
TOTAL TIME: 35 min.

Ingredients

- 1 tablespoon olive oil
- 1 tablespoon unsalted butter
- 1/2 cup shallot, minced
- 1/2 cup celery, minced
- 2 tablespoons dry white wine
- 1 cup medium-grain risotto rice
- 2 tablespoons medium-grain risotto rice
- 3 cups chicken stock or 3 cups meat stock or 3 cups vegetable stock
- 1 1/2 cups peas (fresh or frozen)
- 2 teaspoons unsalted butter
- 2 tablespoons heavy cream
- 1/4 cup parmesan cheese

Instructions

1. Set rice cooker to Cook. Place olive oil and butter in rice cooker. When butter melts, add shallots and celery. Cook until the shallots are softened but not browned, 2 to 3 minutes, stirring occasionally. Add wine and cook for a few minutes. Add rice and stir to coat grains with the hot butter.
2. Cook until rice grains are transparent except for a white spot on each, 3-5 minutes stirring occasionally. Add stock and peas (if fresh), stirring to combine.
3. Close cover and set to Cook. When the machine switches to Warm cycle, stir rice with a plastic or wooden rice paddle. The rice should be al dente.
4. Cook for a few minutes longer if needed. When ready to serve, add peas (if frozen or very tender fresh ones) and stir to combine.
5. Add butter and close the lid for 2-3 minutes to allow butter to melt and the peas are heated through. Stir in cream, cheese, and salt to taste.
6. Serve immediately.

Caribbean Rice

SERVINGS: 4
PREP TIME: 15 min.
TOTAL TIME: 40 min.

Ingredients

- 1 cup white rice, rinsed
- 1 teaspoon ground Jamaican jerk spice or seasoning
- 1/4 cup cilantro or 1/4 cup parsley
- 1 sprig thyme, stem discarded
- 1 garlic clove, minced
- 1 teaspoon grated fresh ginger
- 2 scallions, sliced
- 3/4 cup finely diced sweet potato
- 1/3 cup toasted coconut
- 1/3 cup raisins
- 1/3 cup diced red pepper
- 1 cup vegetable broth, to cover rice

Instructions

1. Place all the ingredients in rice cooker, except for 1 tablespoon scallions and 1 teaspoon coconut which should be saved for garnish. Pour broth 3/4 inch above the level of the rice. Press the cook button.
2. When cooked, fluff with fork. Place in a serving dish and top with reserved coconut and scallions. Place lime alongside for garnish.

Mexican Green Rice

SERVINGS: 4
PREP TIME: 10 min.
TOTAL TIME: 55 min.

Ingredients

- 1 tablespoon unsalted butter
- 1/2 small white onion, chopped
- 1 cup long grain white rice
- 1 1/2 cups water
- 1/2 teaspoon salt
- 1/2 cup fresh cilantro leaves, minced

Instructions

1. Set rice cooker to Cook or regular/Brown Rice cycle. Place butter in rice cooker bowl. When melted, add the onion. Cook and stir until onion is softened and translucent, about 5 minutes. Add rice, water, salt and cilantro to the rice cooker bowl. Stir to combine.
2. Close cover and reset for the regular/Brown Rice cycle or allow previous cycle to complete.
3. When the machine switches over to the Warm cycle, let the rice steam for 15 minutes.
4. Fluff rice with wooden or plastic rice paddle. Serve hot.

Easy Coconut Rice

SERVINGS: 4
PREP TIME: 5 min.
TOTAL TIME: 35 min.

Ingredients

- 2 cups coconut milk
- 2 3/4 cups water
- 2 cups rice
- 1 teaspoon salt

Instructions

1. Clean and wash the rice. Place all ingredients in rice cooker and set to Cook.
2. After it switches to warm, let stand 10 minutes to steam.
3. Serve warm.

Vegetable Rice Pilaf

SERVINGS: 6
PREP TIME: 20 min.
TOTAL TIME: 1 hour 10 min

Ingredients

- 3 teaspoons vegetable bouillon granules
- 3 1/2 cups water
- 3 cups uncooked white rice
- 4 small heads baby bok choy, trimmed and chopped
- 3 green onions, chopped
- 1 carrot, chopped
- 4 mushrooms, chopped
- 1 teaspoon vegetable bouillon granules
- 1/4 cup water, or more if needed
- ground black pepper to taste

Instructions

1. In the rice cooker, dissolve 3 teaspoons bouillon in 3 1/2 cups water.
2. Stir rice, baby bok choy, green onions, carrot, and mushrooms into the bouillon and water mixture.
3. Start rice cooker and cook until liquid is absorbed and rice is tender, around 50 minutes.
4. In a small bowl dissolve 1 teaspoon bouillon and 1/4 cup water. Transfer mixture to a blender.
5. Scoop about 1 cup of the rice mixture into the blender with the bouillon mixture. Blend until mixture becomes a thin paste. Add more water as needed.
6. Mix rice paste with remaining cooked vegetables and rice until thoroughly combined.
7. Season with black pepper.

Quick and Easy Spinach Rice

SERVINGS: 4
PREP TIME: 10 min.
TOTAL TIME: 45 min

Ingredients

- 1 tablespoon vegetable oil, or as needed
- 1 teaspoon cumin seeds
- 1 small onion, minced
- 1 large carrot, minced
- 4 green chile peppers, chopped
- 1 teaspoon ginger-garlic paste
- 1 1/2 cups fresh spinach
- 2 cups uncooked white rice
- 1 teaspoon roasted coriander powder
- 1 pinch salt, or to taste
- 4 1/2 cups water, or more as needed

Instructions

1. Heat oil over medium heat in a skillet. Add and stir cumin seeds until fragrant, about 1 minute. Add onion, carrot, and green chile peppers. Cook and stir until slightly tender, about 5 minutes. Add ginger-garlic powder and cook for about 5 minutes.
2. In a blender, pulse spinach leaves until it turns into a paste. Add spinach paste to onion mixture. Cook and stir until water has evaporated from the spinach, about 2 to 3 minutes.
3. Mix and combine rice, coriander powder, and salt into spinach mixture. Transfer rice mixture to a rice cooker and add water. Press the Cook button.

Chile Cheese Rice

SERVINGS: 8
PREP TIME: 10 min.
TOTAL TIME: 25 min.

Ingredients

- 2 cups white rice, using rice cooker cups
- 3 cups water or 3 cups vegetable broth
- 1 (4 ounce) can diced green chilies
- 1/2 medium onion, diced
- 2 teaspoons garlic
- 1 cup Monterey jack cheese, shredded
- 1 tablespoon margarine

Instructions

1. Sauté onion and garlic in margarine in a small saucepan over medium heat, until onion becomes translucent.
2. Place rice, sautéed onion and garlic, chilies, and chicken broth in rice cooker. Stir to combine. Set cooker to Cook setting. When cooked, mix in shredded cheese and let sit 5-10 minutes.

Toasted Coconut Yellow Rice

SERVINGS: 8
PREP TIME: 10 min.
TOTAL TIME: 45 min.

Ingredients

- 2 cups white rice, thoroughly rinsed
- 1 (14 ounce) can coconut milk
- 1 1/4 cups water
- 1/4 cup sweetened flaked coconut, divided
- 1 teaspoon ground turmeric
- 1/2 teaspoon kosher salt

Instructions

1. Place rinsed rice into rice cooker.
2. Combine and stir coconut milk, water, half of the flaked coconut, turmeric, and salt in a small saucepan. Place over medium-high heat and cook until turmeric is dissolved in the milk mixture and the color is uniform. Pour coconut milk mixture over the rice.
3. Press Start and cook until the cycle completes, about 25 minutes. Leave rice on Warm for 5 minutes.
4. Heat a small skillet over medium-high heat. Toast remaining coconut in skillet until golden brown, about 5 minutes.
5. Fluff cooked rice. Sprinkle toasted coconut over the rice and serve.

Wild Berry Rice

SERVINGS: 4
PREP TIME: 5 min.
TOTAL TIME: 25 min.

Ingredients

- 1 1/2 cups short-grain white rice
- 2 cups water
- 45 ml honey, warmed
- 2 tablespoons butter, melted
- 1 cup cream
- 1 cup mixed berry (fresh or frozen)
- 1/4 cup icing sugar
- 1/4 cup water
- 2 tablespoons port wine (optional)
- berries, for serving

Instructions

1. Place rice and 2 cups water into rice cooker. Cover and set on Cook.
2. Fluff rice and stir in honey, butter and cream. Close lid and allow to stand to for 10 minutes on Warm setting.
3. In a food processer place berries, icing sugar, 1/4 cup water and port and process until smooth. Fold berry mix through rice mix.
4. Transfer to serving glasses and top with extra berries and cream.

Brown Rice with Miso

SERVINGS: 4
PREP TIME: 2 min.
TOTAL TIME: 35 min

Ingredients

- 1 1/2 tablespoons miso (white or yellow)
- 2 1/4 cups water or 2 1/4 cups vegetable stock
- 1 inch fresh gingerroot, peeled
- 2 teaspoons lemon juice
- 1 cup brown rice

Instructions

1. Dissolve miso in 1/4 cup of the water. Combine dissolved miso and the rest of the ingredients in the rice cooker bowl.
2. Set to brown rice or regular Cook cycle. When it switches to Warm cycle, let stand for 15 minutes. Then fluff rice with the plastic paddle or a wooden spoon.
3. Discard ginger and serve.

Saffron & Fruit Chutney Yellow Rice

SERVINGS: 6
PREP/TOTAL TIME: 5 min.
TOTAL TIME: 35 min.

Ingredients

- 3 cups basmati rice, rinsed
- 3 cups water, to the rice cooker level
- 1 pinch powdered saffron (about 5 - 8 strands) or 1 pinch saffron strand (about 5 - 8 strands)
- 2 tablespoons fruit chutney
- 2 -4 cardamom pods, split & use seeds
- salt and pepper
- 1 ounce butter
- 2 -4 sprigs fresh coriander, optional

Instructions

1. Place 3 cups of rinsed Basmati rice in rice cooker, using cup provided. Fill up with water to the 3 cup level. Add saffron, cardamom seeds, salt, pepper & chutney to the rice and water. Using the special non-stick spatula, gently mix. Turn on to the Cook cycle.
2. When ready to serve, add the butter and gently combine. Garnish with chopped fresh coriander/cilantro. Top with some toasted flaked almonds.

Sushi Rice

SERVINGS: 12
PREP TIME: 20 min.
TOTAL TIME: 35 min.

Ingredients

- 3 cups medium grain rice
- 3 1/4 cups water
- 1/3 cup seasoned rice vinegar (to taste)

Instructions

1. Place rice and water in rice cooker. Push button to start cooking.
2. After it is done cooking and it switches to warm, let rice sit in the cooker for about 15 minutes without opening the lid to allow complete steaming. Put rice into a separate bowl and pour vinegar over rice. Gently toss and mix with rice paddle, careful not to mash the rice grains.
3. Use in rolls, sushi or to accompany sashimi.

Rice and Black Beans

SERVINGS: 4
PREP TIME: 5 min.
TOTAL TIME: 35 min.

Ingredients

- 1 cup uncooked rice
- 1 can (10 ounce) diced tomatoes with green chilies (Rotel)
- 1 can (14 1/2 ounce) vegetable broth
- 1 can (15 1/4 ounce) black beans
- 1 can (14 3/4 ounce) sweet corn (optional)
- 1 cup cheese (optional)

Instructions

1. Drain tomatoes, black beans, and corn. Place in rice cooker. Add rice, chicken broth and stir. Cook until cooker stops.
2. Top with cheese and serve.

Easy Jambalaya Curry

SERVINGS: 4
PREP TIME: 5 min.
TOTAL TIME: 50 min.

Ingredients

- 2 tablespoons oil
- 1 cup chopped onion
- 1 tablespoon minced garlic
- 2 tablespoons curry powder
- 2 cups water
- 1 (8 ounce) can tomato sauce
- 1 (8 ounce) package jambalaya mix
- 1/2 cup golden raisin
- 3/4 cup plain yogurt
- 1/3 cup chopped cashews

Instructions

1. Hit Cook and place oil in rice cooker. Add onion and garlic; and cook and stir 5 minutes or until onion is tender. Add curry powder. Cook and stir another 2 minutes.
2. Add water, tomato sauce, Jambalaya Mix, and raisins mix well. Close Lid and hit Cook. After cooker switches to Warm, turn off the cooker and stir in yogurt.
3. Let stand 5 minutes. Sprinkle with cashews.

Polynesian Rice

SERVINGS: 4
PREP TIME: 10 min.
TOTAL TIME: 45 min.

Ingredients

- 1 cup long grain rice
- 1 1/2 cups water
- 1 tablespoon water
- 1/4 teaspoon salt
- 1/4 teaspoon pepper
- 2 teaspoons curry powder
- 1 green onion, minced
- 1/2 cup pineapple, chopped
- 1 cup seedless grapes
- 1/4 cup green bell pepper, seeded and minced
- 1 cup cucumber, diced, for garnish
- 1 lime, cut into wedges, for garnish

Instructions

1. Spray rice cooker bowl with cooking spray or coat with vegetable oil.
2. Put first 6 ingredients (rice to curry powder) in rice cooker. Stir with paddle. Cover and set for regular Cook cycle.
3. When rice cooker switches to Warm, sprinkle green onion, pineapple, grapes (or cherries), and green pepper on top. Cover and let steam for 15 minutes. Stir rice with plastic rice paddle.
4. Garnish with cucumber and lime wedges. Serve.

Quick and Easy Curry Rice

SERVINGS: 5
PREP TIME: 5 min.
TOTAL TIME: 20 min.

Ingredients

- 2 cups uncooked white rice, rinsed
- 3 cups water
- 3 tablespoons mild curry powder

Instructions

1. Stir rice, water, and curry powder together in rice cooker. Cook for a full cycle or until all water is absorbed, about 15 to 20 minutes.

Non-Rice Dishes

Rice Cooker Mac & Cheese

SERVINGS: 4
PREP TIME: 5 min.
TOTAL TIME: 40 min.

Ingredients

- 2 cups pasta
- 1 1/2 cups vegetable stock
- 1 teaspoon salt
- 1 cup whole milk
- 1 1/2 cups shredded cheese

Instructions

1. Place the first three ingredients in the rice cooker and cook for 15 minutes.
2. Add milk and cheese, stir to combine. Close lid and cook for an additional 20 minutes
3. Serve warm.

Very Cheesy Polenta

SERVINGS: 4
PREP TIME: 10 min.
TOTAL TIME: 40 min.

Ingredients

- 2 tablespoons butter
- 1/2 onion, chopped
- 1 clove garlic, minced
- 1 cup vegetable broth
- 1 cup milk
- 1/2 cup polenta
- 1/4 teaspoon salt, or more to taste
- 2 ounces shredded Cheddar cheese
- 2 ounces shredded Parmesan cheese
- 1/4 teaspoon freshly ground black pepper

Instructions

1. Place butter, onion, and garlic in rice cooker. Cover and set cooker on. Cook until onion is soft and translucent, about 10 to 15 minutes, stirring occasionally.
2. Add broth, milk, polenta, and salt. Cover and cook on full cycle, occasionally stirring until polenta absorbs the liquid, around 20 minutes.
3. Add Cheddar cheese, Parmesan cheese, and black pepper. Stir until cheese is melted.

Steamed Tofu & Asparagus

SERVINGS: 4
PREP TIME: 15 min.
TOTAL TIME: 35 min.

Ingredients

- 1/2 small asparagus bunch, 1 1/2-inch lengths
- 1/2 (6 oz.) fried tofu, cubed
- 1/2 small carrot, peeled, thinly sliced
- 1 clove garlic, minced
- 1 tablespoon Aloha Shoyu
- 1 teaspoon vegetable oil
- 1 teaspoon sesame seed oil
- 1 teaspoon mirin
- 1 teaspoon honey

Instructions

1. Toss and combine all ingredients in rice cooker. Turn on rice cooker to cook.

Southwest-Style Quinoa

SERVINGS: 10
PREP TIME: 10 min.
TOTAL TIME: 1 hour 10 min.

Ingredients

- 2 cans (15 ounce) black beans, rinsed and drained
- 2 cans (10 ounce) diced tomatoes with green chile peppers, undrained
- 1 box (12 ounce) quinoa
- 2 cups water
- 1 package (1.25 ounce) dry taco seasoning mix

Instructions

1. Combine black beans, diced tomatoes with green chile peppers, quinoa, water, and taco seasoning in a rice cooker.
2. Cook quinoa mixture on the "brown rice" setting if you have it, or just the regular Cook setting, about 1 hour.

Kimchi

SERVINGS: 4
PREP/ TOTAL TIME: 3 days

Ingredients

- 1 small Napa cabbage (1 lb), cut in half and sliced into 1/2 inch slices
- 1 daikon radish, julienned
- 6 Thai chiles, minced
- 2 cloves garlic, minced
- 1/2 cup green onions, cut into 1/2 inch pieces
- 2 tablespoons ginger, grated
- 1/2 cup coarse sea salt
- 2 tablespoons unseasoned rice vinegar
- 1 teaspoon sugar

Instructions

1. Fill the rice cooker with 2 cups of water and add the salt. Add cabbage and stir making sure it is well coated. Cover and let sit for 24 hours, occasionally stirring.
2. Drain cabbage and add in the rest of the ingredients. Transfer to an airtight canning jar and seal well. Let sit for 3 days at room temperature. Make sure cabbage is covered with pickling liquid by turning upside down.

Rice Cooker Quinoa

SERVINGS: 4
PREP TIME: 2 min.
TOTAL TIME: 20 min.

Ingredients

- 1 cup quinoa
- 2 cups liquid (low-sodium vegetable broth, or water)
- 1/2 teaspoon salt

Instructions

1. Rinse 1 cup of quinoa in cold water. Pour rinsed quinoa into rice cooker.
2. Add liquid and salt. Turn on your rice cooker.
3. Allow quinoa to set for 3 to 5 minutes. Fluff with a fork and serve.

Cheesy Paprika Mac 'n Cheese

SERVINGS: 3
PREP TIME: 10 min.
TOTAL TIME: 40 min.

Ingredients

- 1 1/2 cups elbow macaroni
- 1 1/2 cups vegetable broth
- 1 cup unsweetened almond milk
- 3/4 cup shredded Cheddar cheese
- 1/2 cup shredded mozzarella cheese
- 1/4 cup grated Parmesan cheese
- 1/4 teaspoon paprika
- salt and ground black pepper, to taste

Instructions

1. Mix macaroni, broth, and almond milk together in the rice cooker. Press the Cook button until macaroni is tender yet firm to the bite, around 30 to 40 minutes.
2. Stir Cheddar cheese, mozzarella cheese, Parmesan cheese, paprika, salt, and pepper into macaroni mix until cheeses are melted.

Pasta Cubano

SERVINGS: 3
PREP TIME: 15 min.
TOTAL TIME: 25 min

Ingredients

- 1 tablespoon olive oil
- 400 grams ground round
- 1 cup minced red or green bell peppers
- 1/2 cup minced onions salt, to taste
- 1 teaspoon ground cumin
- 1 teaspoon dried oregano
- 2 tablespoons Worcestershire sauce
- 2 cups water
- 1 cup canned diced tomatoes
- 2 tablespoons sliced green olives
- 1 teaspoon olive oil
- 2 cups uncooked elbow macaroni or penne
- grated Parmesan cheese, for topping

Instructions

1. Heat olive oil in a medium pan. Add ground round and cook until browned. Add and sauté bell peppers and minced onions, until fragrant and soft. Season with salt, cumin, and oregano. Remove from heat. Add Worcestershire sauce.
2. Transfer beef mixture to the rice cooker. Add and mix in water, diced tomatoes, olives, olive oil, and uncooked pasta. Turn on the rice cooker.
3. Check the pasta when it switches to the warm setting. If pasta is not yet cooked, add more water and turn the rice cooker on again.
4. To avoid the pasta becoming soft, do not leave the rice cooker on warm for a long time.
5. Once pasta is al dente, transfer to serving plate and top with cheese.

Quinoa Pomegranate salad

SERVINGS: 4
PREP/ TOTAL TIME: 35 min.

Ingredients

- 2 cups quinoa, rinsed
- 4 cups water pinch of salt
- 1 cup pomegranate seeds
- 1/2 teaspoon all spice powder
- 1/2 cup chopped fresh mint
- 1 tablespoon pine nuts, toasted
- squeeze of lemon juice
- 1 teaspoon olive oil
- salt and cracked black pepper, to taste

Instructions

1. Place quinoa, water and a pinch of salt in the rice cooker. Turn it on.
2. Toast pine nuts while you wait.
3. When quinoa is done, combine all spice and lemon juice. Let it cool.
4. Add all other ingredients and combine.

Potato Salad

SERVINGS: 6
PREP TIME: 10 min.
TOTAL TIME: 30 min. + refrigeration

Ingredients

- 1 1/2 lbs small potatoes
- 1 1/2 cups water, for rice cooker
- 1 1/2 cups mayonnaise
- 1 tablespoon extra-virgin olive oil
- 1 -2 tablespoon vinegar
- 1 teaspoon celery seed
- 2 tablespoons chopped onions
- 1 -2 stalk celery, chopped
- 2 teaspoons prepared mustard
- 1 -2 tablespoon pickle relish
- 1/2 teaspoon salt, to taste
- 2 -4 hard-boiled eggs, coarsely chopped
- Paprika, for garnish

Instructions

1. Cut potatoes into bite size pieces and place in rice cooker with water. Turn rice cooker on Cook and cook for 10-15 minutes, or until potatoes are done.
2. Place rice cooker pan in sink and run cold water in the pan to cool potatoes and eggs. Drain well.
3. Put potatoes in a bowl or container and add the rest of the ingredients. Combine well and refrigerate.

Black Bean Chili

SERVINGS: 6
PREP TIME: 10 min.
TOTAL TIME: 55 min.

Ingredients

- 1 tablespoon olive oil
- 2 carrots diced
- 1/2 onion diced
- 2 cloves crushed garlic
- 2 cans black beans, drained and rinsed
- 1 can black beans, undrained
- 2 tablespoons chili powder
- 1 tablespoon cumin
- 1 can vegetarian refried black beans
- 1 large can of chopped tomatoes
- 1 cup vegetable broth
- pinch of salt
- shredded cheddar
- chopped avocado

Instructions

1. In large pot over medium heat, sauté onions and olive oil and cook until translucent. Add carrots and garlic, and cook until carrots soften. Transfer to a rice cooker and add broth, tomatoes, cumin and chili powder. Start your rice cooker.
2. After it has cooked, add black beans and cook for another cook cycle. When the second cycle is done, add refried beans and combine. Leave rice cooker on Warm to allow refried beans to come up to temperature.
3. Serve with cheddar cheese and avocado.

Rice Cooker Polenta

SERVINGS: 4
PREP TIME: 5 min.
TOTAL TIME: 20 min.

Ingredients

- 1 cup cornmeal (polenta)
- 3 cups water
- 1/4 cup parmesan cheese, grated
- 3 green onions, finely chopped, optional
- 1 tablespoon olive oil
- 1/2 teaspoon oregano
- 1/2 teaspoon basil
- 1/2 teaspoon thyme
- 1/4 teaspoon marjoram
- 1/4 teaspoon sage

Instructions

1. Place all ingredients in rice cooker. Start cooking cycle.
2. After cycle is complete, wait 10 minutes and allow polenta to absorb all the liquid.
3. Stir well before serving.

Rice Cooker Quinoa

SERVINGS: 2
PREP/TOTAL TIME: 20 min.

Ingredients

- 3/4 cup quinoa
- water
- 2 drops olive oil
- salt (suggested 1/4 of a tea spoon)

Instructions

1. Place quinoa in rice cooker. Fill with filtered water per rice cooker instruction.
2. Add olive oil and salt.
3. Set to Cook until it switches to Warm setting.

Jamaican Grits

SERVINGS: 2
PREP TIME: 5 min.
TOTAL TIME: 40 min.

Ingredients

- 16 ounces hominy
- 2 cups water
- 1/2 cup grits
- 1 cup cheese
- 1 teaspoon salt
- 1/4 teaspoon garlic powder
- 2 ounces pimientos

Instructions

1. Add hominy, grits, and water to rice cooker, and press Cook.
2. When on Warm setting, add pimento juice, spices, and cheese until cheese melts.

DESSERTS

Gingerbread Cake

SERVINGS: 8
PREP TIME: 5 min.
TOTAL TIME: 1 hour 15 min.

Ingredients

- 1 1/2 cups white flour
- 1/4 cup sugar
- 1 teaspoon baking soda
- 1/4 teaspoon salt
- 1/2 teaspoon cinnamon
- 3 teaspoons ginger powder
- 1/3 cup oil
- 1/2 cup un-sulphured molasses
- 1 tablespoon vinegar
- 3/4 cup water

Instructions

1. Combine all dry ingredients well. Add oil, molasses, vinegar, and water in the same order. Stir batter until smooth, about 1 minute.
2. Oil or spray cooker spray inside of rice cooker bowl. Pour batter mix in rice cooker. Set to slow or regular cycle. If possible set timer for one hour. (Cooker will shut off after 5 minutes to Warm, restart to Cook cycle and 'bake' for about an hour or until a tooth pick comes out clean from middle of cake). Check progress at 45 minutes, since some rice cookers are faster than others. When toothpick comes clean, turn off.
3. Remove from rice cooker and allow cake to cool 15 minutes in bowl. After cooling put serving dish over top of the cooker bowl and quickly turn over. Transfer cake from bowl to serving dish.
4. Serve warm or cold, topped with puree from canned pears.

Rice Pudding

SERVINGS: 8
PREP TIME: 10 min.
TOTAL TIME: 40 min.

Ingredients

- 5 1/2 cups skim milk
- 2 cups short-grain white rice
- 1 cup white sugar
- 1/2 teaspoon ground cinnamon
- 2 1/2 cups skim milk

Instructions

1. Place 5 1/2 cups skim milk, rice, sugar, and cinnamon in a rice cooker. Stir to combine.
2. Cover and cook for one cycle in rice cooker until rice is creamy and tender, about 20 minutes.
3. Stir in remaining 2 1/2 cup milk.
4. Allow to cool before serving.

Coconut-Pecan Upside Down Cake

SERVINGS: 4
PREP TIME: 5 min.
TOTAL TIME: 45 min

Ingredients

- 1/2 cup butter, softened
- 1/2 cup dark brown sugar
- 1/2 cup shredded coconut
- 2/3 cup chopped pecans
- 1/2 cup semi-sweet chocolate
- 2 tablespoons milk
- 1 (9 ounce) box of yellow cake mix or 0.5 (18 1/4 ounce) box cake mix

Instructions

1. Melt butter in rice cooker. Spray with cooking spray or use parchment paper on bottom of pan. Combine brown sugar, coconut, pecan's and semi-sweet chocolates with a bit of milk. Spread over the butter. Mix up cake mix according to the directions on the box.
2. Hit Cook, it should take around 40 minutes. Turn off and wait a few minutes before removing the pan from the rice cooker.
3. Turn cake over and allow to cool before cutting.

Apple Rice Pudding

SERVINGS: 4
PREP TIME: 20 min.
TOTAL TIME: 40 min.

Ingredients

- 2 cups apples, peeled, cored, and diced
- 1 cup short-grain white rice
- 3 cups water
- 1/2 teaspoon salt
- 1 cup raisins
- 1 pinch nutmeg
- 1 (14 ounce) can sweetened condensed milk
- 4 tablespoons butter
- 1 1/2 tablespoons vanilla

Instructions

1. Put rice, salt, boiling water, raisins, apples, and nutmeg in rice cooker. Turn on to Cook setting. When it switches to Warm, stir in the condensed milk, vanilla, and butter. Turn on to Cook again.
2. Check pudding when it switches to Warm. Set to cook again if there is too much liquid.
3. Garnish with cinnamon.

Chocolate Cake

SERVINGS: 12
PREP TIME: 5 min.
TOTAL TIME: 1 hour 5 min

Ingredients

- 1 1/2 cups white flour
- 1/2 cup raw sugar
- 4 tablespoons dark cocoa
- 1 teaspoon baking soda
- 1/2 teaspoon salt
- 1/2 teaspoon cinnamon
- 1/4 teaspoon double-acting baking powder
- 90 ml sunflower oil
- 1/2 teaspoon vanilla
- 1 tablespoon vinegar
- 1 cup water

Instructions

1. Add and mix together the dry ingredients. Add wet ingredients to the mixture, mixing well until smooth, around 1 minute. Pour batter into the greased rice cooker bowl.
2. Set rice cooker to Slow for 60 minutes, if it doesn't have one just use the regular Cook cycle. If rice cooker goes to Warm cycle, allow to be in that mode for a few minutes then restart timer for remainder time to equal 60 minutes total cook time. Check at 45 minutes.
3. When a toothpick comes out clean from edges and center of cake, it is cooked.
4. Take bowl out when cake is finished, and allow to cool for 15 minutes. Remove cake by inverting bowl on serving plate.
5. Sprinkle with powdered sugar or top with your favourite frosting.

THANK YOU

Thank you for checking out the Quick and Easy Vegetarian Rice Cooker Meals Cookbook. I hope you enjoyed these recipes as much as I have. I am always looking for feedback on how to improve, so if you have any questions, suggestions, or comments please send me an email at susan.evans.author@gmail.com. Also, if you enjoyed the book would you consider leaving on honest review? As a new author, they help me out in a big way. Thanks again, and have fun cooking!

Check out more cookbooks:

Vegetarian Mediterranean Cookbook:
Over 50 recipes for appetizers, salads, dips, and main dishes

Quick & Easy Asian Vegetarian Cookbook:
Over 50 recipes for stir fries, rice, noodles, and appetizers

Vegetarian Slow Cooker Cookbook:
Over 75 recipes for meals, soups, stews, desserts, and sides

Quick & Easy Vegan Desserts Cookbook:
Over 80 delicious recipes for cakes, cupcakes, brownies, cookies, fudge, pies, candy, and so much more!

Quick & Easy Microwave Meals:
Over 50 recipes for breakfast, snacks, meals and desserts

Halloween Cookbook:
80 Ghoulish recipes for appetizers, meals, drinks, and desserts

Printed in Great Britain
by Amazon